Miam...
The ... ouse

Illustrated by **Paolo D'Altan**

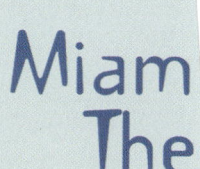

Editor: Michela Bruzzo
Design and art direction: Nadia Maestri
Computer graphics: Simona Corniola
Picture research: Laura Lagomarsino

© 2007   Black Cat

First edition: January 2007

We would be happy to receive your comments
and suggestions, and give you any other
information concerning our material.
info@blackcat-cideb.com
blackcat-cideb.com

CISQ

CISQ CERT

**TEXTBOOKS AND
TEACHING MATERIALS**

The quality of the publisher's
design, production and sales processes has
been certified to the standard of
UNI EN ISO 9001

ISBN 978-88-530-0604-2 Book + audio CD/CD-ROM

Printed in Italy by Italgrafica, Novara

The CD contains an audio section (the recording of the text) and a CD-ROM section (additional fun games and activities that practise the four skills).
- To listen to the recording, insert the CD into your CD player and it will play as normal. You can also listen to the recording on your computer, by opening your usual CD player program.
- If you put the CD directly into the CD-ROM drive, the software will open automatically.

SYSTEM REQUIREMENTS for CD-ROM	
PC:	**Macintosh:**
- Intel Pentium II processor or above (Intel Pentium III recommended) - Windows 98,ME,2000 or XP - 64 Mb RAM (32 Mb RAM Memory free for the application) - SVGA monitor 800x600 screen 16 bit - Windows compatible 12X CD-ROM drive (24X recommended) - Audio card with speakers or headphones	- Power PC G3 processor or above (G4 recommended) - Mac OS 9.0 with CarbonLib or OSX - 64 Mb RAM (32 Mb RAM free for the application) - 800x600 screen resolution with thousands of colours - CD-ROM Drive 12X (24X recommended) - Speakers or headphones
All the trademarks above are copyright.	

Contents

This story is recorded in full.

These symbols indicate the beginning and end of the extracts
linked to the listening activities.

Introduction

This story takes place in Montego Bay near Miami, on the east coast of Florida. Florida is a big peninsula surrounded by the Atlantic Ocean and the Gulf of Mexico. It has a long and interesting history.

The Characters

Bill

Michelle

Francisco Garcìa

Sergeant Walters

Nick

Rover

Montego High School

Montego Bay is a beautiful tourist town on the east coast of Florida, near Miami Beach. The town was founded in the seventeenth century by the pirates of the Caribbean Sea, who were called "buccaneers". Montego Bay became their home port, and there are still legends about hidden treasure there.

The new Montego Bay Wax [1] Museum opened recently. It is a big tourist attraction with wax statues of famous explorers, buccaneers, sea captains, slave merchants [2] and criminals.

Our story starts one Friday morning in October at the Martins' home. Bill and Michelle Martin lived with their parents in a nice old house.

Bill was a tall boy of sixteen, with brown hair and blue eyes.

---

1. **Wax** : candles are made from this.
2. **slave merchants** : men who bought and sold slaves between the 16th and 19th centuries.

This was his third year at Montego High School. Science was his favorite subject and he wanted to become a biologist. Basketball was his sport and he was one of the best players on the school team.

His sister Michelle was a pretty girl of fifteen with short red hair and blue eyes. She loved all kinds of modern music and had a big collection of CDs. This was her second year at Montego High, and she was a member of the Journalism Club, which published the monthly school paper.

"Hurry up, Michelle! It's late!" shouted Bill from the living room.

"I'm coming!" shouted Michelle from the top of the stairs. She ran down and took her backpack. "Bye, Mom! See you this afternoon."

"Bye, Mom!" said Bill. "There's basketball practice today. See you at dinner."

"Enjoy your visit to the new museum!" said their mother. Their father worked at the airport and he was already at work.

Bill and Michelle met their good friend Nick Chan in front of the park. He was a tall Chinese-American of sixteen; he was a member of the basketball team too.

"Hi, guys!" said Nick smiling. "Let's hope this visit to the new wax museum won't be boring."

"I know," said Bill, "and we have to write a report about it for Mrs Jenkins."

The students of the second and third year were visiting the new museum that morning. It was part of their local history course with the new history teacher, Mrs Jenkins. The old teacher, Mr O'Nell, disappeared mysteriously before the

Miami Police File: The O'Nell Case

summer. He was one of the favorite teachers at Montego High, because he was friendly and his classes were interesting.

One day in June Mr O'Nell went out on his boat, the *North Star*. He sailed east to the Bahamas and into the Bermuda Triangle. No one knew why he was going there. The Coast Guard found his boat a few days later, but he was missing [1] — only his dog was on the boat. They took the *North Star* back to the Montego Bay Port and left it there.

The Miami police said Peter O'Nell was missing, because his body was never found. They opened a police file and gave it a number: *File Number 113: The O'Nell Case*. Where was Peter O'Nell? No one knew — it was a mystery.

The local newspaper *The Miami Times* wrote a lot of articles about the "O'Nell Case." The last one said:

Peter O'Nell, another victim of the Triangle?

July 10 – A month after the disappearance of Peter O'Nell, the police are still trying to solve the case. The 45-year – old history teacher and expert scuba diver [2] disappeared during a boat ride in the waters of the Bermuda Triangle.

Police Sergeant Robert Walters says, "People, boats and airplanes often disappear in the Triangle and no one knows why. Could Peter O'Nell be another victim of the Triangle? However, the case is still open. We hope to have an answer one day."

---

1. **missing** : cannot be found anywhere.

2. **scuba diver** :

Bill, Michelle and Nick met their friends and teachers outside the museum. There were a lot of rooms and exhibits with wax statues. There were also models of old Spanish sailing ships and maps of the Caribbean Islands on the walls.

"These statues scare me," said Michelle. "They look like real people."

"You're right," said Juanita, one of Michelle's friends. "Those glass eyes give me the creeps." [1]

"Look at that one," said Nick laughing. "He looks like Mr

---

1. **give me the creeps** : American expression that means "scare me horribly".

Miami Police File: The O'Nell Case

Branson, our math teacher. Look at the small beard and the green eyes."

"Ugh, Mr Branson and his math tests...," said Bill.

"Hey, look at this slave merchant with the red bandana and the black patch [1] over his eye," said Michelle. "He's got a strange tattoo on his arm. I didn't know there were tattoos in those days."

When they left the museum they saw a beagle [2] outside the entrance. He wanted to get into the museum.

"I guess he can't read the sign," said Bill, pointing to the "Dogs not allowed" sign. His friends laughed as they walked to school.

After a long hour of history, it was time for lunch. The school cafeteria was always a noisy, fun place for the students. It was the best time of the day to meet with friends and chat.

Michelle always had lunch with her best friends Juanita and Susan. They usually talked about clothes and boys.

"Michelle, look, there's Matt!" whispered [3] Susan.

"And he's wearing a cool blue sweater," whispered Juanita.

Matt Andersen was the handsome captain of the football team. He was seventeen and Michelle liked him.

She looked at him but he didn't see her, so she started eating her lunch.

"Let's talk about something else, girls!" she said, eating her sandwich.

1. **patch :**    2. **beagle :**     3. **whispered :** said very quietly.

Go back to the text

1 **Comprehension check**

Are these sentences "Right" (A) or "Wrong" (B)? If there is not enough information to answer "Right" (A) or "Wrong" (B), choose "Doesn't say" (C). There is an example at the beginning (0).

0 Montego Bay was founded by buccaneers at the end of the eighteenth century.
A Right   (B) Wrong   C Doesn't say

1 The Montego Wax Museum is a big tourist attraction that opened in September.
A Right   B Wrong   C Doesn't say

2 Bill Martin and Nick Chan play basketball on the high school team.
A Right   B Wrong   C Doesn't say

3 Mrs Jenkins is the new history teacher at Montego High.
A Right   B Wrong   C Doesn't say

4 The Coast Guard could not find Mr O'Nell's boat in the Bermuda Triangle.
A Right   B Wrong   C Doesn't say

5 Sergeant Robert Walters says the O'Nell case is still open.
A Right   B Wrong   C Doesn't say

6 The Montego Wax Museum was small and did not have any exhibits.
A Right   B Wrong   C Doesn't say

7 Mr Branson was the oldest math teacher at Montego High.
A Right   B Wrong   C Doesn't say

8 Michelle likes the captain of the football team.
A Right   B Wrong   C Doesn't say

9 She is having a salad for lunch.
A Right   B Wrong   C Doesn't say

2 Characters

Look at the pictures of Michelle, Bill and Nick on pages 5 and 10 and describe them. Use the words or phrases in the box and write a few sentences about each one.

tall   plays basketball   loves modern music   blue eyes   brown hair   fifteen   black hair   collects CDs   sixteen   pretty   likes science   member of the Journalism Club   Chinese-American   short red hair

1 Michelle: ....

2 Bill: ....

3 Nick: ....

Now describe your best friend in the same way.

3 Vocabulary

Circle the word that doesn't belong and give a reason.

1 town   city   port   village
2 basketball   football   volleyball   club
3 sister   neighbor   brother   daughter
4 lunch   history   math   science
5 boat   airplane   captain   train
6 legend   newspaper   tale   story

Now find the words that don't belong in the word square below and circle them.

```
B  F  Y  N  U  G  O  N  B  Y  H  Z
N  R  U  C  A  P  T  A  I  N  L  H
E  I  P  D  S  Y  V  F  H  A  C  I
W  D  D  O  D  G  T  X  N  N  U  H
S  K  R  J  R  A  M  C  U  I  C  K
P  V  C  G  F  T  I  L  R  V  L  E
A  W  N  C  H  C  J  P  K  A  U  S
P  N  E  I  G  H  B  O  R  D  B  G
E  O  V  H  X  V  S  A  N  X  R  O
R  Z  O  U  K  N  I  M  F  T  Y  S
```

Before you read

1 **Vocabulary**

Match the words in the box with the pictures. Use a dictionary if necessary.

pier	cabin cruiser	scuba diving equipment
fishing net	yacht	fishing boat

1   2   3

4   5   6

Now complete these sentences using one of the words above.

1   The fishermen went to sea in their ....

2   They used a .... to catch fish.

3   Bill and Michelle stood on the .... and looked at the sea.

4   The rich rock star had a beautiful ....

5   Peter O'Nell's boat was a ....

6   He used .... to go underwater.

CHAPTER **TWO**

At the Port

Saturday was a busy day for Bill and Michelle. They both had part-time jobs to earn some pocket money. [1] Bill worked at the local supermarket and Michelle took the neighbors' dogs for walks.

Saturday night was special because Mrs Martin always cooked something unusual. After dinner Michelle went to Juanita's house and Bill phoned Nick.

"What are you doing tonight?" asked Bill.

"As soon as I finish working, I'm going to the movies," said Nick.

"Good idea! What's on?" said Bill.

"There's a science fiction movie at the Madison Theater that everybody's talking about: *Fifth Dimension*. We can meet at my parents' restaurant at half past eight."

---

1. **pocket money** : a small amount of money to buy personal things.

"OK! See you then, Nick."

Nick's parents had a Chinese restaurant near the port and he always worked there on weekends.

As Bill waited for Nick at the back door of the restaurant, he saw the same beagle from the wax museum. The poor dog was sad and thin. He was probably waiting for some food. Nick came out from the back door and said, "What an evening! There was a birthday dinner and we were so busy."

"What's that dog doing there?" asked Bill.

"Oh, him," said Nick. "He's a stray [1] and wants something to eat. My mother always gives him some food. I think he lost his master."

On Sunday morning the port was very busy. People were going out in their boats and the fishermen were repairing their fishing nets.

The Martins had a small cabin cruiser at the port. They decided to clean it because Bill and Michelle wanted to have a Halloween party there.

"Mom and I are going down to the port to clean the boat," said Mr Martin. "You can come later. We can use four extra hands!"

"OK, Dad, we'll be there soon," said Bill.

"I'm going to wear my new jeans and pink T-shirt," said Michelle, who loved wearing new clothes.

"You don't need new clothes to clean a boat, silly," said Bill.

"Boys will never understand!" said Michelle with a smile.

---

1. **stray** : a dog without a master.

Miami Police File: The O'Nell Case

It was almost ten o'clock when Bill and Michelle got to the port. There were always a lot of fishing boats, cabin cruisers, and yachts at the port. It was a warm, sunny day and everything looked beautiful.

An old fisherman, Francisco García, was sitting on a pier near his boat, repairing a fishing net.

"Hi, Francisco!" said Michelle.

"Hello!" said the old man with lively dark eyes. "Nice to see you."

"Are you going out fishing today?" asked Bill.

"No, I'm going early tomorrow morning," he said, looking at his fishing boat. "There he is again, poor thing."

"Who?" asked Bill and Michelle.

"Peter O'Nell's dog, Rover. He sits in front of his master's boat every day and whimpers. [1] Can't you see him?" Bill and Michelle turned around. It was the same dog Bill saw at the museum and at the restaurant.

"Do you mean the beagle over there, near the boat?" asked Michelle, pointing to the *North Star*.

"Yeah," said Francisco. "He's sad because he lost his master. It breaks my heart. I wanted to take him home with me, but he only wants his master."

"The poor dog!" said Bill. "Did the Police ever find Mr O'Nell's body?"

"The Bermuda Triangle took him," said Francisco. "The police will never find his body in the Triangle. He was unlucky, very unlucky, but I told him."

---

1. **whimpers** : cries (crying sounds made by a dog because he's unhappy).

Miami Police File: The O'Nell Case

"What did you tell him?" asked Bill.

"Well, when Mr O'Nell bought the boat he changed its name to *North Star*. I told him it was bad luck to change the name of a boat. Sailors and fishermen know that. But he didn't believe me. He thought it was an old superstition." [1]

"I didn't know that," said Michelle. "But why did he go out to sea that day in June?"

"He brought his scuba diving equipment on board. I think he was looking for something in the sea — something important. He went out in his boat every weekend."

"Did anyone go with him?" asked Bill.

"Only his dog," he said, and his busy hands started repairing the net again.

"It was nice talking to you Francisco — goodbye," said Bill, walking away with Michelle.

"The O'Nell case is a big mystery. No one knows what happened to him and no one knows what he was looking for. We just know that he was a terrific teacher and everyone liked him."

"Well, Francisco thought he was looking for something important," replied Michelle.

"Yeah, but I wonder what?" said Bill.

---

1. **superstition** : when someone believes that particular actions or objects are lucky or unlucky.

Go back to the text

KET **1** **Comprehension check**

Read the sentences below about Chapter Two and put a tick (✓) in the correct box, A, B or C.

1   On Saturday night Bill and Nick
    A   ☐   went to eat at a Chinese restaurant.
    B   ☐   went to a birthday party.
    C   ☐   went to the movies.

2   The Martins went to the port
    A   ☐   to clean their boat.
    B   ☐   to have a Halloween party.
    C   ☐   to see their friends.

3   Peter O'Nell's dog sat in front of the *North Star* and whimpered because
    A   ☐   he was hungry and thirsty.
    B   ☐   he lost his master and he was very sad.
    C   ☐   he wanted to go to Francisco García's home.

4   Francisco García knew Peter O'Nell. He said to him,
    A   ☐   "There is pirate treasure in the Bermuda Triangle."
    B   ☐   "It is dangerous to go to the Bermuda Triangle."
    C   ☐   "It is bad luck to change the name of a boat."

5   Every weekend Peter O'Nell and his dog
    A   ☐   went to sea on the *North Star*.
    B   ☐   went to talk with Francisco Garcìa.
    C   ☐   went for a long walk around the port.

6   The O'Nell case was a mystery because
    A   ☐   nobody knew what happened to him.
    B   ☐   he was a very good swimmer.
    C   ☐   his wife disappeared too.

2 Listening

Listen to the interview between a newspaper reporter and Francisco García. For questions 1-4, put a tick (✓) under the right answer. There is an example at the beginning (0).

0 What newspaper does Jennifer Ross work for?

A ☐

B ☐

C ✓

1 How old is Francisco?

A ☐

B ☐

C ☐

2 Where does Francisco come from?

A ☐

B ☐

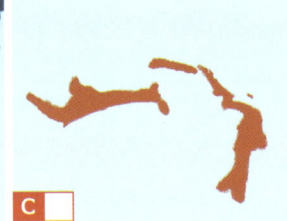

C ☐

3 Where does he live?

A ☐

B ☐

C ☐

4 What time does he get up to go fishing?

| A | B | C |

Before you read

1 Listening

Listen to the first part of Chapter Three. For questions 1-4, tick (✓) A, B or C.

1 Bill and Michelle wore Halloween costumes of

   A ☐ a vampire and a rock star.

   B ☐ a monster and a rock star.

   C ☐ a singer and a ghost.

2 For the Halloween party Mrs Martin made

   A ☐ pumpkin pies and sandwiches.

   B ☐ Halloween cookies and chocolate cake.

   C ☐ pumpkin pies and Halloween cookies.

3 Nick took pictures with his new digital camera

   A ☐ before midnight.

   B ☐ at midnight.

   C ☐ after midnight.

4 The next day Bill and Michelle got up

   A ☐ at eleven o'clock.

   B ☐ at half past twelve.

   C ☐ at twelve o'clock.

CHAPTER **THREE**

A Halloween Party

Saturday October 31 was Halloween and the town of Montego Bay was ready to celebrate it. There were jack-o'-lanterns [1] and black and orange decorations everywhere. There were some incredible costumes in town and people were busy planning scary Halloween parties.

Bill and Michelle planned their costumes and masks weeks before Halloween. Bill was a vampire and Michelle was a rock star. She was excited because she could wear more make-up on Halloween.

They went to the port and had their Halloween party on the boat with their friends. Mrs Martin made pumpkin pies and Halloween cookies and there were good CDs to dance to.

Before midnight Nick took some pictures with his new digital camera. The party was a lot of fun and everyone loved it. No one got to bed before 3 a.m.

Bill and Michelle slept until noon [2] the next day.

"How was the Halloween party?" asked Mr Martin.

---

1. **jack-o'-lanterns** :   2. **noon** : 12 o'clock in the middle of the day.

Miami Police File: The O'Nell Case

"Oh, we had a great time, Dad," said Bill. "Thanks for letting us use the boat."

"We even cleaned up," said Michelle proudly.

"I'm glad you had fun," said Mrs Martin.

That afternoon they went to Nick's house to see the pictures he took the night before.

"Come upstairs and see the pictures of the party!" said Nick excitedly as he opened the door.

"Why are you excited?" asked Michelle. "Is something wrong with them?"

"You both look super," he said. "But that's not the problem — it's something else."

They sat down in front of Nick's computer and started looking at the pictures.

"Look at this one," said Nick. "Can you see the big white spot? It's on the boat in the background."

They looked at the pictures of the party and saw a white spot on a boat in the background.

"Let's look closer at the picture," said Michelle. "I want to see the name of the boat."

"It's the *North Star*!" cried Bill. "It was Mr O'Nell's boat!"

"But what's that white spot?" asked Nick.

They looked at the computer for a while and then Michelle cried out, "I know! It's somebody's ghost in the picture! I read about it in a book. And last night was Halloween — strange things can happen on Halloween night."

"A ghost?" whispered Bill and Nick. "What are you saying?"

"That white spot is the picture of a ghost!" exclaimed Michelle. "And it's on Mr O'Nell's boat, the *North Star*."

"Oh, come on, Michelle!" said Bill, whose face was white.

Miami Police File: The O'Nell Case

"Do you mean that it's... Mr O'Nell's ghost?" Nick felt cold.

"Can you see the... ghost in other pictures?" asked Michelle.

"Well, look at these," said Nick. They looked at three other pictures that had the same white spot on the same boat.

"Wait a minute!" said Bill nervously. "Do we believe in... *ghosts*?" The three friends looked at each other and didn't know what to say.

"Do you have another explanation?" said Michelle, who believed in ghosts.

"Gee!" said Bill. "Then Mr O'Nell is... *dead* and not missing." There was a moment of silence, and then he told Nick about his conversation with Francisco García.

"What happened to him on that day in June?" asked Nick. "Did he have an accident? Or was it bad luck? Francisco said it's bad luck to change the name of a boat."

"Do you believe in superstition and bad luck?" asked Bill.

"I think good and evil [1] forces exist," said Nick seriously.

"Ghosts only appear when the person was murdered or died in a terrible way," said Michelle.

"Perhaps he was looking for something important, and someone killed him to get the information," said Bill.

"But, where's his body?" asked Nick.

"We should tell the Police about this," said Bill.

"The Police don't believe in ghosts," said Michelle. "Why don't *we* try to solve this mystery?"

"Why not!" said Bill. "I like solving mysteries."

"And I like investigating," said Nick. "But we need more information about Mr O'Nell. What was he looking for and why was it important? Let's plan this carefully."

---

1. **evil** : very bad.

Go back to the text

1 Comprehension check

Complete the following sentences (1-6). Choose from the endings A-F.

1 ☐ Bill and Michelle had a great Halloween party
2 ☐ Nick took pictures at the party
3 ☐ Some of the pictures were strange
4 ☐ The big white spot was on
5 ☐ Michelle thought the white spot was
6 ☐ The three friends decided

A the boat in the background — the *North Star*.
B a picture of Mr O'Nell's ghost.
C with his new digital camera.
D on their parents' cabin cruiser.
E to investigate and solve the mystery.
F because they had a big white spot on them.

KET 2 Fill in the gaps

Complete these letters. Write ONE word for each space. There is an example at the beginning (0).

Dear Michelle,

How was (0) .your.... Halloween party? My sister (1) .... I had a small party (2) .... the garden. We put orange and black decorations (3) .... the trees. Everyone had a scary costume. I was a ghost! Tell me (4) .... your party.

        Love, Liz

Dear Liz,

Bill and I had (5) .... great party. (6) .... parents let us use the cabin cruiser. We danced all evening and Nick took pictures (7) .... his new digital camera. The party finished (8) .... two in the morning! (9) .... love Halloween! Come and visit when you're in Florida.

        Love, Michelle

3 Question words

Write the correct question word (*How, Why, Who, When, What, Where*) in the spaces. Then match a question (1-5) to an answer (A-F). There is an example at the beginning (0).

0 .Why.... was Michelle excited on Halloween night?

1 .... do the people in Montego Bay celebrate Halloween?

2 .... did Nick take the pictures?

3 .... did Michelle and Bill go on Sunday afternoon?

4 .... is the name of the boat in the background?

5 .... believes in ghosts?

A ☐ To Nick's house.
B ☐ Before midnight.
C ☐ Michelle does.
D ☐ The *North Star*.
E ☐ They put up decorations and have scary parties.
F ☑ Because she could wear more make-up.

4 Detective work

Are you a good detective? What do you think happened to Peter O'Nell? Choose one of the following and explain why.

A He was a victim of bad luck because he changed the name of the boat.

B He disappeared in the waters of the Bermuda Triangle.

C Someone killed him.

D He had an accident at sea.

E He left Montego Bay and went to live in another part of the United States.

F He lost his memory and could not remember who he was or where he lived.

Before you read

KET ① Vocabulary

Read the definitions. What is the word for each one? The first letter is already there. There is one space for each other letter in the word. There is an example at the beginning (0).

0 It's on top of a house r <u>o</u> <u>o</u> <u>f</u>

1 A big room under a house b _ _ _ _ _ _ _

2 You walk up and down them s _ _ _ _ _

3 You enter the house through this f _ _ _ _ _ _ _ _

4 This is made of wood and you find it around a garden f _ _ _ _

5 Cars are kept in this g _ _ _ _ _

② Vocabulary

Match these words to the different parts of the house.

1 roof   **2** stairs   **3** basement

4 front door   **5** garage   **6** fence

Halloween

Halloween is an important and exciting festivity in the United States, and almost everyone celebrates it. Halloween is becoming popular in other countries because it's a lot of fun.

The Origins

The origins of Halloween go back very far, to the ancient Celts. The Celts lived in the British Isles after 600 BC and they were pagans. They believed in the gods of nature.

Beltane and Samhain were two important festivals on the Celtic calendar. Beltane celebrated the beginning of summer and Samhain celebrated the beginning of winter, on November 1. The festival of Samhain began on October 31 and ended on November 1.

The Celts believed that on the night of October 31 the spirits of the dead came out of their tombs, and they were afraid. They dressed in scary costumes and made big fires to frighten the evil spirits.

The Druids were Celtic religious leaders and teachers. They practiced magic as part of their religious ceremonies. Samhain was an important day for the Druids. They led the celebrations and predicted the future.

The colors of Halloween, orange and black, are of Celtic origin too. Orange was the color of the harvest [1] and black was the color of long winter nights.

Many years after the Roman invasion of Britain in AD 43, Christian

1. **harvest** : the time when farmers collect food from the fields.

Druids meeting for the summer solstice at Stonehenge.

practices substituted pagan festivals. Christians celebrated All Saints'
Day or All Hallows'[1] Day on November 1. The evening of October
31 was All Hallows' Eve, and this became Halloween.

The Druid religion continued for a long time in Scotland and Ireland,
and people continued celebrating Halloween. When Irish
immigrants went to the United States in the 1800s they took their
Halloween traditions to America.

1.   **Hallows** : this is another word for Saints.

Halloween today

Americans love celebrating Halloween. There are orange and black decorations and jack-o'-lanterns everywhere – on streets, in shops, restaurants and schools. People put them in the windows of their homes or outside the front door.

Children, teenagers and many adults wear Halloween costumes and masks. Most costumes are scary – ghosts, skeletons, witches, vampires, monsters, aliens and bats.

Young children bring their costumes to school and have a Halloween party with games in the afternoon. The best costume wins a prize.

Trick-Or-Treaters on Halloween.

Teenage girls at a Halloween Party.

Some older students have a Halloween party and dance in the school gym. Others have parties at their homes and someone tells a spooky [1] story.

Favorite Halloween foods are pumpkin pie, apples, licorice, popcorn and nuts. The favorite Halloween drink is apple juice because the Celts believed apples were lucky.

"Trick-or-treating" is another fun Halloween custom. American children and teenagers go "trick-or-treating" on Halloween night. They go from house to house in their neighborhood and ring doorbells. Then they say "trick-or-treat!" People usually give them candy or money. If people don't, they play tricks on them – they throw an egg at the front door of the house or write on the windows with soap.

1. **spooky** : (American) very mysterious and scary.

1 Comprehension check

Are these sentences true (T) or false (F)? Correct the false ones.

		T	F
1	Halloween is only celebrated in the United States.	☐	☐
2	Halloween has ancient Celtic origins.	☐	☐
3	The Druids dressed in orange and black costumes on Halloween night.	☐	☐
4	The evening of October 31 was called All Hallows' Eve.	☐	☐
5	Irish immigrants took their Halloween traditions to the United States.	☐	☐
6	The Celts believed "trick-or-treating" was lucky.	☐	☐

 INTERNET PROJECT

Connect to the Internet and go to www.blackcat-cideb.com or www.cideb.it . Insert the title or part of the title of the book into our search engine.

Open the page for *Miami Police File: The O'Nell Case*. Click on the Internet project link. Go down the page until you find the title of this book and click on the link for this project.

Divide the class into two groups. Find out more about the Halloween traditions of jack-o'-lantern and trick-or-treating. Write a brief report to present to the class.

Now imagine you have to organize a Halloween party for your class. Choose your favorite costumes, games and food.

CHAPTER FOUR

The Wardrobe [1]

Nick's room was the perfect place to plan things.

"Let's find out more about Mr O'Nell," said Bill. "Where did he live?"

"I'll look it up in the phone directory," said Michelle. "Here it is — his address was 1857 Stockton Street. That's behind the port. Let's try and get into his house."

"But I'm sure the police already went there," said Nick.

"Yeah, but perhaps they didn't examine everything," said Bill. "Let's go there after dark with our flashlights." [2]

"When?" asked Nick excitedly.

"How about Tuesday after dinner?" said Bill.

When the school bell rang at 3.30 p.m. on Tuesday afternoon, Bill, Michelle and Nick hurried home. They did some homework and met at seven.

1. **Wardrobe :**   2. **flashlights :**

Miami Police File: The O'Nell Case

It was a windy autumn evening. They walked to the old part of town and Peter O'Nell's house appeared behind some tall trees. It was a white wooden house with a brown roof and a small garden. They were surprised to see his dog sitting outside the door. He recognized Nick from the restaurant and went to him.

"Look who's here!" said Nick smiling. "Hi, Rover! What are you doing here?"

"He's still looking for his master," said Bill.

"He's friendly," said Michelle stroking[1] him.

"Let's go to the back of the house and see if the door is open," said Nick.

Rover followed them. The back door was locked so they opened the kitchen window and climbed in.

They stood in the dark kitchen for a moment — everything was silent.

"We're in Mr O'Nell's house!" said Bill. "This is weird!"[2]

"Let's start looking for clues,"[3] said Michelle.

"Where can we start?" asked Nick.

"Look, Rover's going to the living room," said Michelle. "Let's follow him."

The living room was small and there were two armchairs near the window. There was a big color photograph of O'Nell and his dog on a small table.

Michelle looked at the photograph. "It was probably taken on his boat in the summer. Look, he's got a strange tattoo on his arm."

"It's a peace sign," said Bill. "They were popular in the 1970s."

1. **stroking :**  2. **weird :** strange, mysterious.

3. **clues :** information that helps you understand a mystery.

Miami Police File: The O'Nell Case

Rover led them to the hall and sat down in front of a door. He barked[1] and put his paw[2] on the door.

"Let's open it," said Michelle.

She was scared, but she opened the door. There were stairs that went to the dark basement and the air was cold. Bill and Nick turned on their flashlights and slowly went down the stairs, and Michelle and Rover followed them. They looked around and saw a few boxes of books, some diving equipment and a big wooden wardrobe. Rover went to sit in front of the old wardrobe and started barking.

"Why is he barking at the wardrobe?" asked Nick as he stroked the dog's head. He barked again and looked at Nick with his big brown eyes. Then he began pushing the wardrobe door with his paw.

"Let's open it," said Nick.

His heart beat fast as he turned the key and opened the door. He saw two scuba diving suits.

"There's nothing interesting in here," he said, closing the wardrobe.

Rover barked again and pushed the door with his paw. Nick opened the wardrobe again and looked inside carefully.

"Could there be something behind this wardrobe?" said Michelle.

"Like in mystery novels, Michelle?" said Nick laughing.

"Yes, exactly!" said Michelle. "Come on, let's try and move it to one side."

"OK, let's try," said Bill. The wooden wardrobe was very heavy but they were able to move it a bit. Rover was right — there was a small opening to a tiny[3] room!

---

1. **barked** : made the typical sound of dogs.
2. **paw** :
3. **tiny** : extremely small.

Go back to the text

KET **1** **Comprehension check**

Read the paragraph below and choose the best word (A, B or C) for each space. There is an example at the beginning (0).

Bill, Michelle and Nick want to find out (**0**) .....C........ about their teacher, Mr O'Nell. They decide to go to his house (**1**) .... Tuesday evening with (**2**) .... flashlights. When they get there they see Rover (**3**) .... at the front door.

The three friends enter the house (**4**) .... the kitchen window and start looking around. They go to the small living room and see a photograph of Mr O'Nell and his dog. Then Rover leads (**5**) .... to the dark basement and sits in front of (**6**) .... old wardrobe. He starts barking loudly. Nick opens the wardrobe and looks inside, (**7**) .... he doesn't find (**8**) .... interesting.

0	**A** many	**B** lot	**C** more
1	**A** on	**B** at	**C** in
2	**A** they're	**B** their	**C** there
3	**A** sat	**B** sitting	**C** sits
4	**A** through	**B** between	**C** at
5	**A** their	**B** they	**C** them
6	**A** the	**B** an	**C** a
7	**A** why	**B** because	**C** but
8	**A** anything	**B** something	**C** nothing

"Perhaps they didn't examine everything."

There are four pronouns that begin with **every-** : **everything, everybody/everyone, everywhere**.

We use **everything** for objects, **everybody/everyone** for people and **everywhere** for places.

2 Indefinite pronouns

Fill in the gaps with *everything*, *everybody/everyone* or *everywhere*.

1 .... was looking at the dog and laughing.

2 The police examined .... in the house carefully.

3 Bill and Nick looked at .... in the basement but they found nothing.

4 .... liked Mr O'Nell at school because he was friendly.

5 Nick's parents traveled .... in Florida during the summer.

6 Michelle told her best friend .... about the Halloween party.

3 Listening

Listen to an interview about beagles and complete the notes.

1 sense of smell ....

2 ears ....

3 legs ....

4 height ....

5 weight ....

6 eyes ....

7 they hunt ....

8 they were the favorite dogs of ....

Before you read

1 Detective work

What do you think Bill, Michelle and Nick will find in the tiny room? Choose one of the following and explain why.

1 nothing

2 more scuba diving equipment

3 a pirate's treasure

4 Mr O'Nell's body

5 something else ....

2 Listening

Listen to the first part of Chapter Five and choose the correct answer, A, B or C.

1 The three friends discovered
- A ☐ a flashlight.
- B ☐ a secret basement.
- C ☐ a secret room.

2 On the walls they saw
- A ☐ some photographs and a map.
- B ☐ some newspaper articles and maps.
- C ☐ a big map of Florida and a letter.

3 Mr O'Nell's boat disappeared
- A ☐ in the Bermuda Triangle.
- B ☐ between Miami and Puerto Rico.
- C ☐ near Mexico.

4 Michelle looked through
- A ☐ the old newspapers.
- B ☐ the phone directory.
- C ☐ Peter O'Nell's diary.

5 Professor Ortega worked for
- A ☐ *The Miami Times*.
- B ☐ the Montego Bay Wax Museum.
- C ☐ the Florida Historical Museum.

6 Mr O'Nell disappeared on
- A ☐ June 15.
- B ☐ June 8.
- C ☐ June 9.

CHAPTER **FIVE**

A Secret Closet[1]

This is super!" said Michelle. "We discovered a secret room!"

"You mean a secret closet," said Nick, moving his flashlight around. "It's very small."

There were two big maps and some newspaper articles on the walls and a diary on an old chair.

"This is cool!" said Bill. "I don't think the police know about this place."

"And it's probably full of clues," said Nick.

The maps on the wall showed the Bermuda Triangle — the sea between Miami, Puerto Rico and Bermuda. There were red pen marks on the maps.

---

1. **Closet** : (American) a very small room.

Miami Police File: The O'Nell Case

"Mr O'Nell was probably trying to find a particular spot in the Bermuda Triangle," said Nick.

"Hmm... listen to this headline from *The Miami Times*," said Michelle. "*Ship with Precious Cargo [1] Disappears in the Bermuda Triangle*"

"Let's see," said Bill holding up his flashlight. The three of them started reading the newspaper article on the wall...

A small ship, *The Pelikan*, disappeared in the Bermuda Triangle last week. It was transporting ancient Roman and Greek artifacts, [2] bought in Europe by an important American museum. The artifacts are worth millions of dollars, and they are now probably sitting on the bottom of the Atlantic Ocean.

"I think I understand," said Bill. "Mr O'Nell was probably looking for the ship in the Bermuda Triangle. That's why these two maps are marked in the same place."

"And that's why he went out in his boat with his diving equipment every weekend," added Michelle.

"But why was he looking for them?" asked Nick.

"That's a good question," said Bill. "I'm sure a lot of dishonest art dealers want to find those artifacts and sell them on the black market... it's a big business! They're worth millions of dollars. But Mr O'Nell wasn't dishonest. I'm sure he was looking for them for another reason."

Michelle started looking through the diary on the chair.

---

1. **Cargo** : objects carried on a ship or plane.
2. **artifacts** : valuable objects of great archaeological and cultural interest.

Miami Police File: The O'Nell Case

"Hey, look!" she said. "On June 7 Mr O'Nell wrote this note in his diary: *'Call Professor Ortega at Florida Historical Museum'*. That's the day before he disappeared."

She paused for a moment and said, "Perhaps Mr O'Nell was working for the Florida Historical Museum and that's why he was looking for the ship."

"That's a good explanation; he was an expert scuba diver," said Bill. "Is there anything else in that diary?"

Michelle looked through the pages.

"On May 31 he wrote, *'Blackbeard still following me at sea.'* "Who's *Blackbeard*?"

"Well, he was a pirate, centuries ago. I don't think it's him," said Nick.

"But *Blackbeard* could be the name of a boat — the boat that was following him. Perhaps the people on that boat were looking for the artifacts too. Let's go to the port and see if the *Blackbeard* is there," said Bill.

"Alright," said Nick, "but let's go now — it's late."

"And it's getting very hot in this closet!" said Michelle.

Suddenly there was a loud noise upstairs.

"What's that?" cried Michelle.

"We're not alone here," said Nick. "Someone or something is in the house!" They stood still for a minute.

"Well, Michelle," whispered Nick, "you're the ghost expert — whose ghost is upstairs?"

"Oh, stop it!" whispered Michelle, who wanted to get out of there.

They got out of the secret closet and quickly pushed the wardrobe against the wall. They went upstairs silently and climbed out of the small kitchen window, followed by Rover. When they were outside the house they heard another loud noise and ran away.

"That math test was impossible!" said Nick, walking out of Mr Branson's class angrily.

"I think he makes math hard for us," said Bill. "I couldn't finish the last two problems."

"Me neither," said Nick. "I studied until late last night, but it didn't help. Even Maria Lopez, who's a math genius, didn't finish the last problem!"

"Hey, let's think about the big game against South Miami High tonight," said Bill. "They're a strong team."

"And so are we!" said Nick.

That evening the Montego High gym was crowded and noisy. The colors of the two schools were everywhere — orange and purple for Montego and black and red for South Miami. It was an important basketball game and the local TV station was there to film it. Michelle sat with Juanita and Susan.

Mike Andersen and his friends from the football team were sitting behind them and this made Michelle nervous. "I'm happy I wore my new sweater with the school colors," she thought. "I hope Mike notices it."

It was an exciting game and everyone was cheering [1] for their team. Montego High finally won and entered the Florida finals.

Someone touched Michelle's shoulder. She turned around and saw Mike.

"Hi, Michelle," said Mike. "Your brother played a great game!"

---

1. **cheering** : (here) shouting loudly to encourage a team.

"Oh, thanks, Mike, I'll tell him," said Michelle, who was happy because Mike talked to her.

On the way home after the game Bill, Michelle and their friends walked by the wax museum. They saw Rover sitting at the entrance. He was whimpering.

"I wonder what Rover's doing in front of the museum at this time?" asked Michelle.

"There's something about the place that attracts him," said Bill. "But what? Remember the day when he tried to come into the museum with our class?"

Go back to the text

KET ① **Comprehension check**

Are these sentences "Right" (A) or "Wrong" (B)? If there is not enough information to answer "Right" (A) or "Wrong" (B), choose "Doesn't say" (C). There is an example at the beginning (O).

O There were red pen marks on the maps on the wall.
(A) Right   **B** Wrong   **C** Doesn't say

1 The ship was transporting three ancient Roman and Greek artifacts.
A Right   **B** Wrong   **C** Doesn't say

2 Michelle found Mr O'Nell's agenda on a chair in the secret closet.
A Right   **B** Wrong   **C** Doesn't say

3 The *Blackbeard* was following Mr O'Nell's boat on June 7.
A Right   **B** Wrong   **C** Doesn't say

4 Michelle forgot to wear her new sweater with the school colors to the game.
A Right   **B** Wrong   **C** Doesn't say

5 Rover was sitting outside the Montego High gym after the basketball game.
A Right   **B** Wrong   **C** Doesn't say

② **The past simple**

When Michelle got home after the basketball game, she wrote about it in her diary. Complete her diary with the past simple tense of the verbs in brackets.

November 13 — Montego High (**1**) .... (*win*) the basketball game tonight and we (**2**) .... (*get*) to the Florida finals. It's wonderful! Bill and Nick (**3**) .... (*play*) a great game and (**4**) .... (*score*) a lot of points for the team.

Mom and Dad (**5**) .... (*be*) happy to be there. They (**6**) ....
(*cheer*) all evening.

I (**7**) .... (*see*) the team's new uniforms for the first time tonight and I really (**8**) .... (*like*) them.

Mike Andersen (**9**) .... (*sit*) behind me and we (**10**) ....
(*talk*) about the game. When the game (**11**) .... (*be*) over Mike
and I (**12**) .... (*go*) for ice cream. He (**13**) .... (*tell*) me
about his football game next week. I hope to go and see it because I
like him! Mike likes to go biking and I do too. He (**14**) .... (*buy*)
a new mountain bike last week. I hope we can go biking together
soon. At eleven o'clock we (**15**) .... (*have*) to go home. What a
great evening!

KET ❸ **Conversation**

**Complete the conversation. What does Mike say to Michelle? Write
the correct letter next to the number. There is an example at the
beginning (0).**

Mike: Hi, Michelle! What are you doing on Saturday night?

0 Michelle: ......B......

Mike. Do you want to come to the movies with me?

1 Michelle: ....

Mike: *The Mummy Returns* at the Madison Theater at eight o'clock.

2 Michelle: ....

Mike: I hope you like scary movies.

3 Michelle: ....

Mike: Good! What time can I pick you up?

4 Michelle: ....

Mike: What time do you have to be back home on Saturday night?

5 Michelle: ....

A No later than midnight.

B Nothing special.

C I can.

D Susan says it's good.

E No, I didn't.

F At half past seven.

G What's on?

H They're my favorites.

T: GRADE 4

4 Speaking: hobbies/sports

Bill and Nick play on the basketball team, and Mike Andersen is the captain of the football team. What is your favorite sport? Tell the class about it and use these questions to help you.

1 Why do you like this sport?

2 How often do you play/watch this sport?

3 Do you prefer team sports or individual sports?

4 What other sports do you play?

 INTERNET PROJECT

Connect to the Internet and go to www.blackcat-cideb.com or www.cideb.it. Insert the title or part of the title of the book into our search engine.

Open the page for *Miami Police File: The O'Nell Case*. Click on the Internet project link. Go down the page until you find the title of this book and click on the link for this project.

American football is extremely popular in the United States. People play the game at high schools, colleges and universities. Professional football is a big business and there are many important professional teams. In pairs, find out more about the sport. Answer the questions below.

▶ What is the object of the game?

▶ What is the game called outside the United States and Canada?

▶ How many teams are there in the National Football League?

▶ What is Super Bowl Sunday?

▶ Do women play football?

American
High School Sports

Sports are an important part of high school life in the United States. American students love sports and are proud to play on the school teams. Some students practice more than one sport. Every high school has a basketball, an American football, baseball and volleyball team. And some schools have a swimming team too.

American high schools have big, modern gyms and vast outdoor sports areas. Some schools even have Olympic-size swimming pools. Students meet after school to train with their team two or three times a week. The trainer or coach is a physical education teacher.

The team usually plays in a local championship on weekends and

Swimming competition in a pool.

Cheerleader at a basketball game.

sometimes on week nights. Games are an important and exciting event. Each school team has a uniform with the school name and colors. There is always a big audience at the games – students, parents and grandparents. The gym is decorated with the school colors and local TV stations often film the games.

Before and during the game a group of five or six girls called cheerleaders lead the cheering. They wear colorful uniforms and are fun to watch.

In June of every year there are prizes for the best athletes and the best teams.

Baseball and basketball

Baseball is the country's national sport. It started from the British ball games rounders and cricket in the late 1700s.

In baseball there are two teams of nine players. The players on one team must hit a hard ball with a wooden bat and run around four markers (the "bases") in a diamond shape.

The first professional baseball team in the United States was the

Cincinnati Red Stockings (1869). Today this team is called The Cincinnati Red Sox. By 1871 there were nine teams in the National Association of Professional Baseball Players. Today almost every city and town has a professional baseball team. Famous American baseball players of the past were Babe Ruth, Lou Gehring, Joe Di Maggio and Willie Mays.

Basketball is also extremely popular. It began in the late 1800s. A physical education teacher, James A. Naismith, invented an indoor game to play during the long, cold winters: basketball.

In a game of basketball there are two teams of five players. Each team tries to win points by throwing a ball through a hoop (also called the "basket").

Many people now play the game all over the United States and in other countries. The National Basketball Association (NBA) started in 1949 and is now the world's biggest professional basketball association. The Los Angeles Lakers are one of American's best teams. Some famous names in American basketball are Michael Jordan, Magic Johnson and Larry Bird.

1 Comprehension check

Are the following questions true (T) or false (F)?

1 American students are proud to play on their school team.

2 All schools have Olympic-size swimming pools.

3 Cheerleaders wear colorful uniforms and lead the cheering.

4 The best athletes and the best teams get prizes every month.

5 America's national sport is basketball.

6 There are five players on a basketball team.

Before you read

1 Listening

Listen to the first part of Chapter Six and decide if the sentences are true (T) or false (F).

		T	F
1	Bill, Nick and Michelle continued investigating the case on Saturday.	☐	☐
2	The Naval Registry Office was at the port.	☐	☐
3	Michelle talked to a fisherman at the office.	☐	☐
4	Mr Devereau was from New Orleans.	☐	☐
5	There was no information about Mr Devereau on the web.	☐	☐
6	Mr Devereau owns a museum in New Orleans.	☐	☐

2 Reading pictures

A   Look at the picture on pages 62 and 63, and answer these questions.

1   Where are Bill and Nick?

2   Why do you think they're hiding?

3   What is the yacht like?

4   Whose sports car do you think is parked on the pier?

B   Now look at the picture on page 65, and answer these questions.

1   What are Bill and Nick doing?

2   Why is Nick holding a flashlight?

3   Where is Bill's flashlight?

4   What is on the table?

5   What do you think they found?

CHAPTER **SIX**

The 'Blackbeard'

O n Sunday Bill, Nick and Michelle continued investigating the case. This time they met in Bill's room.

"We have to find the *Blackbeard* and see who it belongs to," said Bill. "I'm sure there's a connection between that boat and Mr O'Nell."

"There's a Naval Registry office at the port," said Michelle. "All boats at the port are listed there."

"Good! Let's go to the port," said Bill.

The Naval Registry was a small office near the Montego Yacht Club. Michelle went in and talked to the clerk. [1]

"Hello, my name is Michelle Martin and I need some information. Is the *Blackbeard* here?"

"Let me check," said the clerk, as he turned to his computer.

---

1. **clerk** : a person who works in a shop or office.

Miami Police File: The O'Nell Case

"Here it is — the *Blackbeard*. It's at pier number eight; that's where the biggest yachts are."

"Can you tell me the name of the owner?"

"Let's see... it's Mr Julian Devereau from New Orleans."

"Julian Devereau!" said Michelle, surprised.

"Yes, Julian Devereau. He and his wife are the owners of the new wax museum."

"OK, thanks for your help," said Michelle.

She met Bill and Nick outside and told them about the *Blackbeard*.

"Wow!" cried Nick.

"So Julian and Gertrude Devereau are the owners of the wax museum and the *Blackbeard*," said Bill.

"And they gave a lot of money for the new park," said Nick.

"There's a connection," said Michelle.

"Why were they following the *North Star* at sea? And what about the wax museum?" asked Nick. "Why is Rover so attracted to it?"

'This case is really difficult,' said Michelle.

"Well," said Bill, "we know that the *Blackbeard* is at the port and that Julian Devereau owns the boat and the wax museum."

There was a moment of silence.

"And we know he's rich," said Nick, "but that's not much."

"The clerk said that Julian Devereau is from New Orleans," added Michelle. "Let's go home and look on the web."

At home they got on the web and found some interesting information.

Devereau was the owner of a maritime museum in Charleston, South Carolina, and a new art museum in Houston, Texas.

The 'Blackbeard'

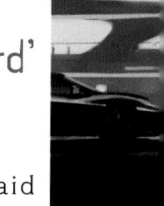

"This man owns three museums — he's very rich," said Michelle grinning. [1] "And guess what you find in museums?"

"Artifacts!" cried Bill and Nick. "Like the ones O'Nell was looking for!"

"Exactly!" said Michelle excitedly.

"So what's the next step?" asked Nick.

"Hmm," said Bill, looking at the computer screen. "We have to find a way to get on the *Blackbeard*. We could find some evidence of Devereau's connection to this mystery."

"The *Blackbeard*'s at pier number eight," said Michelle. "We can go one evening when the museum is open. I don't want to meet them face to face!"

"The museum's always open on Friday and Saturday evenings until 10 p.m.," said Nick, "and the Devereaus are there on those evenings."

"OK!" said Bill. "Listen to my plan. On Friday night Nick and I will try to get on the *Blackbeard*. Michelle, you can sit in the coffee shop across the street from the museum. If the Devereaus leave the building, call me on my cell phone." [2]

"Good plan!" said Nick.

It was November and almost Thanksgiving, [3] but the three friends could only think about the O'Nell case.

On Friday evening they met in front of the museum. It was cold and windy, and Michelle ordered a cup of hot cocoa at the coffee shop. She watched the museum entrance with her cell phone in her hand, ready to make a call.

---

1. **grinning** : a grin is a big smile that shows the teeth.
2. **cell phone** : American for mobile phone.
3. **Thanksgiving** : American festivity that remembers the first Pilgrims of 1620. On this day families meet and have a big meal together.

There was no one at the port that evening. The boys could hear their footsteps as they walked quickly past the *North Star* and turned left at pier number eight. The lights of the *Blackbeard* were on and the two boys stopped behind a van. [1]

1. van :

"Someone's on the boat," whispered Nick. "What shall we do now?"

"Let's wait here and see what happens," said Bill.

Suddenly the lights went off. Julian Devereau got off the yacht and into his sports car and drove away.

Miami Police File: The O'Nell Case

"Whew!" said Bill. They waited a few minutes and then got on the yacht. The glass door was closed but not locked, so it was easy to get in.

"He didn't lock it. He's probably coming back soon," said Nick. "Let's hurry!"

They turned on their flashlights. It was their first time on a yacht — everything was beautiful and expensive. They started looking everywhere — drawers, cupboards, bookshelves — but they couldn't find anything.

Bill took a painting off the wall and turned it around, but he found nothing. He did the same with another painting and this time there was an envelope on the back.

"Nick, look at this!" Bill opened the envelope; inside there was a map of the Florida coast and the Bermuda Triangle, with some red pencil marks. It was almost identical to the maps in Mr O'Nell's house.

"The Devereaus have Mr O'Nell's map, and they hid it behind a painting," said Nick, staring at the map.

"This is evidence that the Devereaus are connected to Mr O'Nell in some way," said Bill. "We have to show this map to the police."

"Will they listen to us?" asked Nick.

"Let's go and find out!" said Bill.

Bill put the empty envelope behind the painting. Then he folded the map and put it in his shirt pocket. They got back onto the pier and quickly left the port. They picked up Michelle, who was still at the coffee shop.

"Hi, guys," she said. "You found something, didn't you!"

"Let's go to Sandy's Ice Cream Parlor and talk there," said Bill.

Go back to the text

1 Comprehension check

Are the following sentences true (T) or false (F)? Correct the false ones.

		T	F
1	The *Blackbeard* was a big fishing boat at pier number eight.	☐	☐
2	Julian and Gertrude Devereau owned the Montego Bay Wax Museum.	☐	☐
3	The Montego Bay Wax Museum didn't close until 10 p.m. on Friday and Saturday evenings.	☐	☐
4	When Bill and Nick got to pier number eight Julian Devereau was not there.	☐	☐
5	The door of the yacht was locked so Bill and Nick broke the glass and went in.	☐	☐
6	Bill found a map of Montego Bay in an envelope behind a painting.	☐	☐
7	Michelle was waiting for Bill and Nick at Sandy's Ice Cream Parlor.	☐	☐

"It's at pier number eight; that's where the biggest yachts are."

Biggest is the superlative of *big*.

To form the superlative of one-syllable adjectives we use **the** and add **-est** to the end of the adjective (rich — *the* rich*est*).

For words with two syllables or more we put **the most** in front of the adjective (*interesting — the most interesting*).

Remember that some adjectives have irregular superlative forms.

2 Superlatives

Complete the table below with the superlative forms of the adjectives. Be careful — two of the adjectives have irregular superlative forms.

	Adjective	Superlative
1	Tall	....
2	Beautiful	....
3	Short	....

4 Poor ....

5 Good ....

6 Old ....

7 Strange ....

8 Bad ....

9 Dangerous ....

Now complete the following sentences using the superlative form of the adjective in brackets. There is an example at the beginning (0).

0 The *Blackbeard* was *the longest* .... (*long*) yacht in the port.

1 Juanita was .... (*fast*) swimmer on the swimming team.

2 Francisco Garcìa was .... (*old*) and ....
   (*nice*) fisherman at the port.

3 Maria was .... (*good*) student in the math class.

4 The .... (*cold*) room in the house was the basement.

5 Julian Devereau owned .... (*important*) art museum in
   Texas.

6 Andrew was the .... (*bad*) player on the football team.

 **3 Notices**

Which notice (A-H) says this (1-5)? There is an example at the beginning (0).

A
> **PIER No. 8**
> **For Yachts 100 ft.**
> **or longer**

B
> **Bikers**
> **not allowed**
> **inside the port**

C
> **Naval Registry Office**
> Open everyday
> 9 am-6 pm
> except Jan. 1

D
> **U.S. COAST GUARD**
> **military area**
> **KEEP OUT!**

E

> Big reduction on all
> Scuba Diving
> Equipment

F

> **Montego Bay Wax Museum**
> **Free entrance for**
> **children under 5**

G

> **Do not park cars**
> **on piers**

H

> Peter's PET SHOP
> closed on Sundays

0 [D] You cannot enter the military area.

1 [ ] You cannot visit this office at 8 o'clock in the morning.

2 [ ] Your four-year-old brother can enter the museum without a ticket.

3 [ ] Leave your bike outside the port.

4 [ ] Diving equipment is cheaper now.

5 [ ] You can buy dogs here from Mondays to Saturdays.

Before you read

1 Listening

Listen to the first part of Chapter Seven and decide if the sentences are true (T) or false (F).

		T	F
1	Bill and Michelle did not go to work on Saturday morning.	☐	☐
2	Mr and Mrs Martin got angry when they heard about what was happening.	☐	☐
3	Sergeant Walters was a tall policeman with friendly eyes.	☐	☐
4	The three friends talked with him for about half an hour.	☐	☐
5	At the police station, the O'Nell case file was number 130.	☐	☐
6	There was no real evidence against Julian and Gertrude Devereau.	☐	☐

CHAPTER **SEVEN**

Sergeant Walters

Before going to their part-time jobs on Saturday  morning, Bill and Michelle told their parents what was happening. Mr and Mrs Martin were very surprised.

"Why didn't you tell us about this before?" said Mrs Martin, who was worried.

"You kids are amazing!" said Mr Martin. "No one has solved this mystery, but perhaps you can. I remember Mr O'Nell — he was a very nice man. I'm glad you're going to the police today. It's the right thing to do."

That afternoon the three friends went to the police station and spoke to a police officer.

"Good morning, I'm Sergeant Walters," said a tall man with friendly eyes. "What can I do for you?"

"We want to report something," said Bill.

"Come into my office and sit down," said Sergeant Walters.

Bill was a bit nervous at first, but Sergeant Walters was friendly. He, Nick and Michelle explained everything. They talked with him for about half an hour, and he seemed interested.

"Sergeant Barnes, please bring me the O'Nell case file, number 113," said Sergeant Walters. He looked through several papers in the file and then wrote something down.

Miami Police File: The O'Nell Case

"You three are good detectives," he said, "but do you know that it is against the law to enter private property, like Mr O'Nell's home and the *Blackbeard*?"

Bill and Nick were embarrassed, but Michelle was not.

"We wanted to help the police solve the case," she said seriously. "We were looking for clues... but we won't do it again."

"The Devereaus are important citizens," said Sergeant Walters. "They helped our community with their new museum and they gave lots of money for the new park. The wax museum brings tourists and good business to our town. We don't have any real evidence against them. You found this map on their yacht, but anyone can have a map."

"But this map is identical to the ones we saw at Mr O'Nell's house, and it was hidden behind a painting," said Nick.

"We want to solve the O'Nell case, too," said Sergeant Walters. "But I need better evidence. For example, where is Mr O'Nell's body? Perhaps he wanted to disappear and start a new life in another place. A lot of people disappear, you know. Or perhaps he had an accident at sea. We can't accuse anyone at the moment. We need to find his body first."

"Mr O'Nell loved his dog," said Michelle. "He could never go away and leave him!"

"Dogs are very good at finding their masters... it's their sense of smell," said Sergeant Walters, with a strange light in his eyes. "My men and I'll examine the secret room in Mr O'Nell's house and take a look at those maps and his diary. But I still think he had an accident. Do you know how many people and boats disappear at sea?"

He got up from his desk and gave each of them his business card. "Call me if you need me."

Sergeant Walters

They left the police station and Bill said, "Now we have to find the body before anyone will listen to us."

"Yeah, bodies are easy to find — they're everywhere, didn't you know?" said Nick, laughing.

"Oh, come on! Don't worry," said Michelle. "Remember what Sergeant Walters said: 'Dogs are good at finding their masters — it's their sense of smell.' I think he's giving us a clue."

"Perhaps Rover can help us solve the case," said Bill.

Nick thought for a moment. "You can usually find him near the *North Star*, or at Mr O'Nell's home, or..."

"Or at the wax museum!" cried Michelle. Her cheeks were red with excitement. "What attracts Rover to the museum?"

"Something inside?" said Bill.

"Yes, but what?" said Michelle.

"Let's find a way to get into the museum with Rover," said Nick. "Dogs aren't allowed in the building, but there's a back door, the emergency exit. One of us can open it and Rover can go in."

"Great idea, Nick!" said Bill.

"We can go tomorrow," said Michelle. "It's Sunday and there are always lots of visitors at the museum — no one will notice Rover... I hope."

"OK," said Bill. "Nick, Rover likes you, so you can wait outside the back door with him. Michelle and I'll buy tickets and go in. When we get to the back of the museum we'll open the door and you and Rover can come in. Then we'll follow the dog and see what happens."

"Good," said Nick. "My mother usually feeds [1] him at nine o'clock. I'll try to keep him at the restaurant tonight."

---

1. **feeds** : gives him food to eat.

Go back to the text

KET ❶ **Comprehension check**

Read the sentences below and then answer the questions. Choose A, B or C.

1 On Saturday afternoon Bill, Michelle and Nick
   A ☐ went to their part-time jobs.
   B ☐ went to the Miami Police Station.
   C ☐ went to the Naval Registry Office.

2 The Devereaus were important citizens of Montego Bay because
   A ☐ they opened a museum and gave money for the new park.
   B ☐ they gave money for the new port.
   C ☐ they were rich.

3 Sergeant Walters wanted to solve the O'Nell case, but first he needed
   A ☐ to talk to Julian Devereau.
   B ☐ to find O'Nell's body.
   C ☐ to examine the secret closet.

4 Bill, Michelle and Nick decided to take Rover
   A ☐ to the police station with them.
   B ☐ to *The North Star*.
   C ☐ to the Montego Bay Wax Museum.

5 Dogs were not allowed inside the museum,
   A ☐ but Rover could go in secretly through the back door.
   B ☐ but Rover could go in secretly though the side window.
   C ☐ so Rover could wait outside the front entrance.

6 Nick's mother usually
   A ☐ worked at the restaurant until nine o'clock.
   B ☐ fed Rover at nine o'clock.
   C ☐ started working at the restaurant at nine o'clock.

74

2 Prepositions

Fill in the gaps with the correct preposition from the box below.

through	during	in	behind	outside	before	on	inside

1 There were a lot of tourists standing in line .... the museum.

2 "Let's phone the police station .... going," said Nick.

3 Rover ran .... the park looking for the ball.

4 Julian Devereau put the map .... the painting.

5 It was hot .... the secret closet.

6 "There was a big storm .... the night so I couldn't sleep," said Nick.

7 "It's Thanksgiving .... Thursday, and Christmas .... about a month!" said Juanita happily.

KET 3 **Writing**

Sergeant Walters writes an email to Tom McKinley, Chief of Police in Miami. Complete the email. Write ONE word for each space. There is an example at the beginning (0).

The O'Nell Case

Send Now Send Later Save as Draft Link ▾ Delete Signature ▾ Options ▾ Insert ▾ Categories ▾

From: Sergeant Bob Walters
To: Tom McKinley
Cc:
Subject: The O'Nell Case
▶ Attachments: none

Font ▾ Size ▾ **B** *I* U T

Hi Tom,

I have some news (0) ...far....... you on the O'Nell Case. Do (1) ....
remember the history teacher at Montego High School who disappeared
last June? It was case number 113. Well, something new and interesting
(2) .... happening here.

Three teenagers (3) .... investigating the case! They're smart [1]
kids (4) .... they want to help the police. I talked with (5) ....
for about half an hour.

They think there's a connection between the owner (6) .... the

---

1. **smart** : (American) clever, intelligent.

Montego Bay Wax Museum and Peter O'Nell. They got (7) ....
Devereau's yacht and found a map of the Bermuda Triangle! I'm
confused now, but (8) .... think we have a big mystery to solve.
Sgt Barnes and I must (9) .... back to O'Nell's house on Stockton
Street and examine a few more things. Perhaps O'Nell wasn't a victim
of the Triangle after all. What (10) .... you think, Tom?

Talk to you soon,

Bob

T: GRADE 3

4 Speaking: places in the local area

The Montego Wax Museum is a place of interest in town. What is your
favorite place of interest in your town or city? Tell the class about it
and use these questions to help you.

1   Describe your favorite place. What do you like about it?

2   How often to you visit it?

3   What do you do when you're there?

4   Do you go alone or with your friends?

Before you read

1 Detective work

What do you think will happen next? Choose one answer and explain
why.

1   The three friends and Rover will find an important clue in the
     museum.

2   They will get into trouble for bringing a dog inside the museum.

3   They won't find an answer in the museum and they will return to
     the *North Star*.

4   There is no answer because O'Nell was a victim of bad luck and the
     Triangle.

CHAPTER **EIGHT**

At the Museum

Bill and Michelle woke up early on Sunday morning. This was a very important day for them and Nick. They left their house at half past nine and met Nick in the park.

"Hi, Nick!" said Bill, looking at Rover's new red leash! [1]

"The leash was my mom's idea," said Nick, as they walked towards the museum. "You and Michelle go ahead and I'll wait for you outside the back door."

That morning a lot of tourists were buying tickets so Bill and Michelle had to wait to get in. They went to the back of the museum and opened the emergency door.

Nick and Rover went in quickly, and no one noticed them. Rover walked to the wax statue of the slave merchant with the black patch over his eye. Rover stopped in front of it and started

1. leash :

sniffing and whimpering — and the noise got louder. Some tourists saw him but they didn't stop.

"I think Rover found something," said Michelle. She and the boys looked at the seventeenth-century slave merchant. Then Michelle noticed the tattoo on the statue's arm.

"Hey, look at that tattoo," whispered Michelle. "Do you

remember it? It's the same tattoo we saw in the photograph at Mr O'Nell's house!"

"The peace sign!" whispered Nick. "But they were popular in the 1970s. A slave merchant of the 1600s didn't know about peace signs!"

Rover started barking.

Miami Police File: The O'Nell Case

"He's found something!" said Bill, as the barking got louder and the dog became more excited.

"Could... *that* be his master?" said Nick, his voice trembling.

"But it's a wax statue," said Michelle weakly.

"Yeah, but look at the tattoo!" said Bill. "Is that a wax statue... or is it someone's *body*?" They felt cold and their hearts started beating fast. Suddenly their legs felt weak.

"But how is it possible..." Nick couldn't finish his sentence.

Rover's bark got louder and the museum guard came by.

"I'm sorry, dogs aren't allowed in the museum," he said. "Please take him out."

"No, we're not taking him out," said Bill angrily.

"You must obey the rules of the museum, or I'll call the police."

"No," said Bill angrily, "we'll call the police! Michelle, do you still have Sergeant Walters's card?"

"Of course I do!" she said, taking out her phone. "I'll call him."

Several visitors stopped to see what was happening. Rover was very excited and barked loudly. Nick pulled on the leash to hold him back.

Michelle called Sergeant Walters and asked him to come immediately. "We have a body for you," she said with a trembling voice. More visitors stopped near them.

Sergeant Walters, Sergeant Barnes and two other policemen got to the museum in a few minutes.

"Sergeant Walters, we found Mr O'Nell's body!" said Michelle loudly. "His dog led us here and started barking. We noticed that the tattoo on the statue is the same tattoo we saw in a photograph at Mr O'Nell's home — a peace sign, popular in the

1970s. And this museum is owned by Mr and Mrs Devereau."

"O'Nell's body?" exclaimed Sergeant Walters. "What are you saying? I want to look into this!" He turned to the museum guard and said, "I want to examine this statue carefully. Do you have a back room?"

"Yes, I'll open it for you," said the guard.

Sergeant Walters asked his men to take the statue to the back room. "I want to speak to the owners of the museum immediately," he said.

"Mr and Mrs Devereau are in their office upstairs. I'll go and call them." The guard was worried and confused.

Sergeant Walters's men carried the statue to the back room, and Rover started following them. Nick pulled him back but it wasn't easy. Sergeant Walters called the police station and asked them to send a medical expert. Then he turned to the three young people, who were very excited about their macabre [1] discovery.

"I don't know what we'll discover here, but something is wrong, and we're going to find out more about that wax statue. Your detective work was excellent and you helped us a lot. But now it's the responsibility of the police. Call me in a few days and I'll tell you something more. Thanks for your help!"

The three friends were proud — they were helping the police solve the O'Nell case!

When they left the museum Nick took the leash off Rover but he didn't run away — he stayed with them.

1. **macabre** : horrible, scary.

Go back to the text

KET **1** **Comprehension check**

Read the paragraph below and choose the best word (A, B or C) for each space (1-9). There is an example at the beginning (0).

(0) ...B......... Sunday morning Bill and Michelle met Nick and Rover in the park. They went to the wax museum. When Bill and Michelle were (1) .... they opened the emergency door for Rover and Nick. Rover went to the statue of the slave merchant and (2) .... loudly.

Michelle noticed the tattoo on the statue's arm and (3) .... the photograph at O'Nell's house. She told Bill and Nick about the photograph and the tattoo.

The three friends suddenly had (4) .... terrible thought: perhaps this was O'Nell's body! They felt cold and (5) .... hearts beat fast. Rover was very excited and (6) .... visitors stopped to see what was happening.

Michelle phoned Sergeant Walters, who came immediately with (7) .... men and decided to examine the statue in the back room of the museum. He wanted (8) .... find out more about the statue.

Sergeant Walters thanked the three friends (9) .... their excellent detective work. Bill, Michelle and Nick left the museum and were proud.

0	**A** In	**B** On	**C** At
1	**A** inside	**B** into	**C** indoors
2	**A** bark	**B** barking	**C** barked
3	**A** saw	**B** thought	**C** remembered
4	**A** a	**B** an	**C** some
5	**A** their	**B** there	**C** the
6	**A** much	**B** several	**C** lots
7	**A** him	**B** his	**C** the
8	**A** of	**B** for	**C** to
9	**A** for	**B** about	**C** of

② Vocabulary

Read the definitions. What is the word for each one? The first letter is already there. There is one space for each other letter in the word. There is an example at the beginning (0).

0   You use it to walk a dog   l e a s h

1   A big, expensive boat   y _ _ _ _

2   You make candles with it   w _ _

3   A dog without the master   s _ _ _ _

4   Very bad   e _ _ _

5   Strange, mysterious   w _ _ _ _

6   A very small room   c _ _ _ _ _

③ Listening

The museum guide at the Montego Bay Wax Museum is talking about pirates to a group of tourists. Listen to the recording and answer the questions below.

1   Who is Janet Cruz?

2   Who were the pirates of the Caribbean Sea?

3   What kind of men were they?

4   How many buccaneers were there in the Caribbean?

5   Where is Port Royal?

6   Who did Jamaica belong to in 1655?

7   Who lived in Port Royal?

8   Who was Henry Morgan?

④ Reading pictures

Look at the picture on page 87 and answer these questions.

1   Why are Michelle, Bill and Nick so happy?

2   What do you think they are reading about in the newspaper?

3   What part of town are they in?

CHAPTER **NINE**

The Case is Solved

Do you think that was really Mr O'Nell's... body?" asked Nick.

"If it was, this is like a horror movie!" said Bill.

"What if the other statues... were bodies?" Michelle said weakly.

"Oh, please, Michelle!" said Nick. "Devereau reminds me of Dr. Frankenstein!"

"When will we find out something?" asked Bill.

"I'm going to call Sergeant Walters in a few days," said Michelle.

Bill, Michelle and Nick did not have to wait long. On Wednesday the O'Nell case was on the front page of *The Miami Times*:

O'Nell Case Finally Solved

The O'Nell Case was finally solved by the Miami Police this week with the help of three teenagers – Bill Martin, 16, his sister Michelle, 15, and Nick Chan, 16. These young people showed great determination and courage.

The police discovered the waxed, embalmed [1] body of Peter O'Nell, a 45-year-old high school teacher and expert scuba diver, in the Montego Bay Wax Museum. The macabre discovery was a big shock for everyone because he went missing in June of this year. The owners of the wax museum, Julian Devereau, 46, and his wife Gertrude, 42, made a terrible confession. They killed Peter O'Nell.

Peter O'Nell was working for Professor Dan Ortega, who is the director of the Florida Historical Museum. Professor Ortega asked him to find the ship with the five artifacts that disappeared in the Bermuda Triangle. The ship left the port of Naples, Italy, but never reached its destination in Miami. All radio contact was lost when the ship entered the Triangle.

The museum bought these valuable artifacts in Greece and Italy to add to its beautiful art collection.

Julian Devereau owns an art museum in Houston and a maritime museum in Charleston. He knew about the lost artifacts and wanted to find them for his museums. He followed O'Nell's boat during his trips to sea. On June 8, when O'Nell was scuba diving, Devereau went on his boat and stole O'Nell's maps. These important maps showed where the ship and the artifacts were.

O'Nell returned to his boat before Devereau could leave it. He shot and killed O'Nell with his gun. With the help of his wife he brought O'Nell's body back to his yacht, the *Blackbeard*. They had to eliminate the body so they took it to the wax museum that night.

Julian Devereau is an expert chemist and he embalmed the body. Then he

---

1. **embalmed** : conserved with chemicals.

Miami Police File: The O'Nell Case

put it in a bath of hot wax and made it look like a statue – the wax statue of a slave merchant of the 1600s. With a patch over one eye, a dark beard and a red bandana it was almost impossible to recognize O'Nell. But the expert chemist forgot to eliminate the tattoo on O'Nell's arm.

With O'Nell's maps Devereau found the five artifacts in the Triangle and hid them in his museum in Houston.

The priceless artifacts will return to the Florida Historical Museum next week. The Montego Bay Wax Museum is closed for now.

On Saturday morning there will be funeral services for Peter O'Nell. All the students and teachers of Montego Bay High School will be present.

O'Nell's dog Rover, who helped to solve this case, found a new home with Nick Chan and his family.

After reading the article several times, Bill, Michelle and Nick couldn't believe that they solved the case. But they were sad about O'Nell's terrible death. Now Michelle had a big story for the December issue of the school paper. She was suddenly the most popular member of the Journalism Club.

"The Devereaus almost committed the perfect crime," she said.

"Yeah, but they forgot about a dog's instinct and his sense of smell," said Bill, grinning at Rover.

"Let's celebrate at my restaurant!" said Nick and Rover barked.

"That's super!" exclaimed Bill.

"Hey, let's walk down to the port and invite Francisco," said Michelle. "After all, he's part of this too... he was the first one to give us clues."

At that moment Michelle's phone rang and she saw Mike's number on the display. Now everything was really perfect.

Go back to the text

KET **1** **Comprehension check**

Read the sentences below and then answer the questions. Choose A, B or C.

1   The O'Nell case was on the front page of
   A ☐ the high school paper.
   B ☐ *The Miami Times.*
   C ☐ *The Florida Times.*

2   Peter O'Nell was working for
   A ☐ the Florida Historical Museum.
   B ☐ Julian Devereau.
   C ☐ the Montego Bay Wax Museum.

3   Julian Devereau owned
   A ☐ a yacht and a museum.
   B ☐ two museums.
   C ☐ a yacht and three museums.

4   Julian Devereau went on O'Nell's boat because
   A ☐ he wanted to talk to Peter O'Nell.
   B ☐ he wanted to steal the artifacts.
   C ☐ he wanted to steal Peter O'Nell's maps.

5   Julian Devereau hid the five artifacts
   A ☐ in his museum in Houston.
   B ☐ in the Montego Bay Wax Museum.
   C ☐ on his yacht, the *Blackbeard.*

6   Devereau forgot
   A ☐ to hide the maps.
   B ☐ to hide the artifacts.
   C ☐ to eliminate the tattoo.

② Crossword

Complete the crossword puzzle with words from the text.

Across

3 a big, expensive boat

8 a festivity on October 31

11 valuable objects of interest

12

13 against the law

14

5 a very small room

6 American festivity in November

7

9 Rover has a new one

10 you take pictures with it

Down

1 Mike's favorite sport

2 Nick's parents have one

4 a picture or design on your body

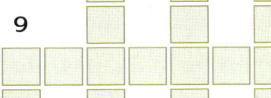

The Bermuda Triangle

The Bermuda Triangle is the area in the Atlantic Ocean between Bermuda, the south coast of Florida and Puerto Rico.

The Bermuda Triangle is often called the Devil's Triangle or the Graveyard [1] of the Atlantic, because strange and mysterious things happen there. Planes, ships and people disappear in the Triangle and no one knows why.

Lost ships

Christopher Columbus was the first person to write about the Bermuda Triangle in his diary. During his sea voyage to the New World in 1492, he saw that his compass [2] did not work in the area of the Bermuda Triangle. He also saw strange red lights in the sky.

---

1. **Graveyard** : a place where dead bodies are put.
2. **compass** : an instrument that shows the direction (north, south, east or west).

For centuries after Columbus's voyage many ships and their crews [1] disappeared in this area of the Atlantic.

On 30 January 1921 the crew of the ship *Deering* disappeared in the Triangle. The ship was in perfect condition but the crew was missing. What happened to them? No one knows.

In 1944 the United States Coast Guard found the ship *Rubicon* on Florida's east coast with no people on it – they only found a small, frightened dog.

In 1963 another big ship called *Marine Sulphur Queen* disappeared during its voyage from Texas to Virginia. No one ever found it.

Lost planes

On 5 December 1945, a group of five United States Navy planes left Fort Lauderdale, Florida. On that day the weather was perfect. After two hours the five planes began flying over the Bermuda Triangle.

Suddenly the instruments on the planes stopped working. The pilots could not communicate with Fort Lauderdale any more. Then the Navy planes disappeared and no one could explain why. The Naval Station sent out search planes to look for them for several days. One search plane disappeared too, and the others could not find the lost planes. Newspapers wrote many articles about the lost Navy planes and their pilots.

What do scientists say about this Triangle? Some say that there are

---

1. **crews** : people who work on a ship or plane.

Five US Navy planes.

often bad weather conditions. Others say that there are strong magnetic fields. [1]

Some people say that there are aliens in the Triangle who kidnap [2] people. But these are not good explanations. The Bermuda Triangle is still a great mystery for everyone.

---

1. **magnetic fields** : places where the earth's magnetic force is very strong.
2. **kidnap** : take away against your will.

Comprehension check

Read the sentences below and then answer the questions. Choose A, B or C.

1 The Bermuda Triangle is in the
- A ☐ Caribbean Sea.
- B ☐ Atlantic Ocean.
- C ☐ Pacific Ocean.

2 It is often called
- A ☐ the Atlantic Triangle.
- B ☐ the Devil's Graveyard.
- C ☐ the Devil's Triangle.

3 In 1492 Christopher Columbus's compass did not work
- A ☐ because there were red lights in the sky.
- B ☐ because it was old.
- C ☐ because he was in the Bermuda Triangle.

4 The United States Coast Guard found the *Rubicon*
- A ☐ in the Bermuda Triangle.
- B ☐ on Florida's west coast.
- C ☐ on Florida's east coast.

5 The Naval Station sent out search planes
- A ☐ and one search plane disappeared.
- B ☐ and they found the pilots.
- C ☐ and they found the lost planes without the pilots.

6 Scientists say there are
- A ☐ aliens in the Triangle.
- B ☐ strong winds in the Triangle.
- C ☐ strong magnetic fields in the Triangle.

KET **1** **Comprehension check**

Are these sentences "Right" (A) or "Wrong" (B)? If there is not enough information to answer "Right" (A) or "Wrong" (B), choose "Doesn't say" (C).

1 The Coast Guard found Peter O'Nell's cabin cruiser near Charleston, South Carolina.

   A Right B Wrong C Doesn't say

2 Peter O'Nell was an expert scuba diver and won three international prizes in the United States and Europe.

   A Right B Wrong C Doesn't say

3 Peter O'Nell changed the name of his cabin cruiser from the *Pelikan* to the *North Star*.

   A Right B Wrong C Doesn't say

4 After looking at the Halloween party pictures, Bill, Michelle and Nick decided that O'Nell was dead.

   A Right B Wrong C Doesn't say

5 Professor Dan Ortega was an important art dealer in Miami and a friend of Gertrude Devereau's.

   A Right B Wrong C Doesn't say

6 Julian Devereau owned a maritime museum in Houston and an art museum in New Orleans.

   A Right B Wrong C Doesn't say

7 Bill and Nick found an important page from O'Nell's diary behind a painting on the *Blackbeard*.

   A Right B Wrong C Doesn't say

8 Sergeant Walters told Bill, Nick and Michelle that it was against the law to enter O'Nell's house and the Devereau's yacht.

   A Right B Wrong C Doesn't say

9 Sergeant Walters asked the medical expert to examine the statue of the slave merchant.

   A Right B Wrong C Doesn't say

10 Julian and Gertrude Devereau killed O'Nell and threw his body in the Atlantic Ocean near the Bahamas.

   A Right B Wrong C Doesn't say

11 Julian Devereau found the artifacts and sold them for three million dollars on the black market.

   A Right B Wrong C Doesn't say

2 Characters

Match each description with a character. You can use the name of some of the characters more than once.

1 ☐ She was Michelle's best friend.
2 ☐ He taught history at Montego High School and the students liked him.
3 ☐ His parents owned a Chinese restaurant near the port.
4 ☐ She was a member of the Journalism Club.
5 ☐ He was the handsome captain of the football team.
6 ☐ He was an old fisherman at the port.
7 ☐ He wanted to become a biologist.
8 ☐ She liked wearing new clothes.
9 ☐ Mrs Chan fed him in the evening.
10 ☐ She was the new history teacher at Montego High.
11 ☐ He took pictures at the Halloween party.
12 ☐ He gave Bill, Nick and Michelle his business card.
13 ☐ She believed in ghosts.
14 ☐ He was an expert chemist.
15 ☐ She loved all kinds of modern music.
16 ☐ He drove a sports car.

A	Bill Martin	G	Mike Andersen
B	Francisco García	H	Juanita
C	Sergeant Walters	I	Julian Devereau
D	Michelle Martin	J	Rover
E	Nick Chan	K	Mrs Jenkins
F	Peter O'Nell		

This reader uses the **EXPANSIVE READING** approach, where the text becomes a springboard to improve language skills and to explore historical background, cultural connections and other topics suggested by the text.

The new structures introduced in this step of our **READING & TRAINING** series are listed below. Naturally, structures from lower steps are included too. For a complete list of structures used over all the six steps, see *The Black Cat Guide to Graded Readers*, which is also downloadable at no cost from our website, blackcat-cideb.com

The vocabulary used at each step is carefully checked against vocabulary lists used for internationally recognised examinations.

Step **One A2**

All the structures used in the previous levels, plus the following:

Verb tenses
Present Simple
Present Continuous
Past Simple
Past Continuous
Future reference: Present Continuous; *going to*; *will*; Present Simple
Present Perfect Simple: indefinite past with *ever*, *never* (for experience)

Verb forms and patterns
Regular and common irregular verbs
Affirmative, negative, interrogative
Imperative: 2nd person; *let's*
Passive forms: Present Simple; Past Simple
Short answers
Infinitives after verbs and adjectives

Gerunds (verb + *-ing*) after prepositions and common verbs
Gerunds (verb + *-ing*) as subjects and objects

Modal verbs
Can: ability; requests; permission
Could: ability; requests
Will: future reference; offers; promises; predictions
Would … like: offers, requests
Shall: suggestions; offers
Should (present and future reference): advice
May (present and future reference): possibility
Must: personal obligation
Mustn't: prohibition
Have (got) to: external obligation
Need: necessity

Types of clause
Co-ordination: *but; and; or; and then*
Subordination (in the Present Simple or Present Continuous) after verbs such as: *to be sure; to know; to think; to believe; to hope; to say; to tell*
Subordination after: *because, when, if* (zero and 1st conditionals)
Defining relative clauses with: *who, which, that*, zero pronoun, *where*

Other
Zero, definite and indefinite articles
Possessive *'s* and *s'*
Countable and uncountable nouns
Some, any; much, many, a lot; (a) little, (a) few; all, every; etc.
Order of adjectives
Comparative and superlative of adjectives (regular and irregular)
Formation and comparative/superlative of adverbs (regular and irregular)

Available at Step **One**: